Junior Seau

by Mark Stewart

ACKNOWLEDGMENTS
The editors wish to thank Junior Seau for his cooperation in preparing this book.
Thanks also to Integrated Sports International for their assistance.

PHOTO CREDITS
All photos courtesy AP/Wide World Photos, Inc. except the following:

Rob Tringali, Jr./Sports Chrome – Cover
Junior Seau – 9, 11, 46 top left
University of Southern California – 13, 14, 16, 22 bottom left
Mark Stewart – 48

STAFF
Project Coordinator: John Sammis, Cronopio Publishing
Series Design Concept: The Sloan Group
Design and Electronic Page Makeup: Jaffe Enterprises, and
         Digital Communications Services, Inc.

LIBRARY OF CONGRESS CATALOGING-IN-PUBLICATION DATA
Stewart, Mark.
   Junior Seau / by Mark Stewart.
     p. cm. – (Grolier all-pro biographies)
   Includes index.
   Summary: A brief biography of the all-pro linebacker for the San Diego Chargers.
   ISBN 0-516-20154-9 (lib. binding)-ISBN 0-516-26010-3 (pbk.)
   1. Seau, Junior, 1969-   –Juvenile literature. 2. Football players–United States–Biography–
Juvenile literature. 3. San Diego Chargers (Football team)–Juvenile literature.
[1. Seau, Junior, 1969- . 2. Football players. 3. Samoan Americans–Biography.]
I. Title. II. Series.
GV939.S393S84   1996
796.332'092–dc20
   [B]   96-12718
                                                                                 CIP
                                                                                  AC

Grolier ALL-PRO Biographies™

Junior Seau

by
Mark Stewart

CHILDREN'S PRESS®
A Division of Grolier Publishing
New York • London • Hong Kong • Sydney
Danbury, Connecticut

Contents

Who

Am I?

There is nothing easy about growing up in a bad neighborhood. Temptation, danger, and hopelessness are everywhere. To get out, you need to work hard, be yourself, and—most importantly—you must have a dream. Mine was to play in the NFL. And there wasn't a single day when I lost sight of where I wanted to be and what I wanted to do. My name is Junior Seau, and this is my story . . . "

"You need to work hard, be yourself, and . . . you must have a dream."

J.R. Seau #55

Growing Up

When Tiaina Seau was just five years old, he boarded a plane in the island nation of American Samoa and settled into his seat for the long journey across the Pacific Ocean to California. He was leaving a place where life was simple and quiet, and he was heading for a poor section of San Diego called Oceanside. There, he would find that just living was hard and the streets were mean. Today, Junior looks back and realizes how fortunate he is to have survived a childhood in a poverty-stricken inner city neighborhood. "I didn't have to read about starvation, drugs, gangs—it was all around my home. I lived it, and it was no fun."

Tiaina had been in the United States when he was an infant, but his parents decided he should not have to grow up surrounded by danger and poverty. They had sent their baby back to Samoa, where he lived with his grandparents. When he returned to California at age five, Tiaina had trouble getting used to his new life. The first thing to change was Tiaina's name. His family started calling him "Junior" because his father's name also was Tiaina.

Back home on the island of Aununu, things had moved very slowly. In California, everything seemed to happen all at once. The Seaus lived in a very small house, and days and nights were very hectic with so many kids running around. In their tiny, two-bedroom home, Junior's two sisters slept in one room, his parents slept in the other, and he and his four brothers shared a room that had once been the garage. Junior's bed was next to a dishwasher and the cabinet where his

Junior stands in front of his older brothers and sisters.

mother kept cleaning supplies. The floor was cold and damp, the roof leaked, and there was no insulation in the walls to keep the boys warm. Junior's parents dreamed of the day when they could afford to move to a bigger house in a safer area. But there never seemed to be enough money, even though both worked very hard. "When we were growing up," Junior remembers, "my family didn't have a lot of money, but we did have a lot of love, and I had my dreams."

Junior's mother, Luisa, worked in a laundromat. His father was a school custodian. They had come to the United States in 1964 after learning that their oldest son, David, had a lung disease that could not be treated by doctors in Samoa. Tiaina ruled the Seau family with a firm hand. He demanded that Samoan be spoken in the house at all times, and he tried to preserve the traditions and culture of his native land. He wanted his children to understand and appreciate their heritage.

Because Junior had never learned English while growing up in Samoa, he had trouble communicating with other children for a couple of years after he moved to California. When he started attending grade school in California, he had a very difficult time. But within two years, he had learned to speak and read English, and he began to improve as a student.

ath came easily to Junior, thanks to his favorite teacher, Mr. Burton. He knew just how to motivate Junior and make him feel good about himself. Mr. Burton also taught him how to play chess, a game that Junior enjoyed because it was like a combination of math and his favorite sport, football. History was Junior's least favorite subject. He had to put in a lot of extra studying to make passing grades. "Without knowledge," Junior says, "you don't go anywhere in this world. And if you

Junior's sixth-grade class photo, including his favorite teacher, Mr. Burton (standing at right). Junior is third from the left in the back row.

can't read, you can't get knowledge. That's why reading is so important—it's the most powerful tool you have."

By the time he reached high school, Junior had blossomed into an A student. He was even selected to the state All-Academic team for his ability to balance the demands of football and schoolwork. In this area he received a bit of help from his father. When Junior was doing his homework, his father—a huge man with a short temper—would chase his friends away when they came to the house. After a while, even Junior's toughest pals were afraid to go near the family's front porch. They would wait quietly in the street until he came outside.

Long before high school, Junior discovered that he had a talent for sports. From baseball to body surfing, he displayed a natural ability at everything he tried. When Junior played with his brothers, however, he was at a disadvantage, because they were much bigger than he was. So he decided to build his body into a sports machine. Junior lifted homemade weights in front of a mirror, did chin-ups on a tree in the backyard, and did countless push-ups on his bedroom floor. Although Junior saw people abusing drugs and alcohol nearly every day of his life, he never used them. Junior was proud of his body and could not imagine poisoning it. His drug was winning.

unior became quite an athlete at Oceanside High School. He played linebacker and tight end for the football team, and he led the Pirates to a city championship in his senior year. Junior was such a dominant player that he was named the league's offensive MVP, and he was chosen as the defensive MVP of the entire San Diego area. *Parade* magazine honored him as a high-school All-American, but because he played so many different positions so well, the magazine did not list him at a single position! Since Junior was also a top student, he could have attended any school in the country on a football scholarship. He chose the University of Southern California (USC), because it was close to home and his family could come and see him play.

College

J unior Seau had his entire life planned out. He would attend Southern California for four years, develop his football skills, and then try for a career in the NFL. Junior decided he would study public administration in college, so that if he did not make it in the pros, he could get a good job in city or state government. But then the unthinkable happened. When Junior took the SAT college

When Junior finally got to play for USC, he chose to wear number 55 to honor his father, who turned 55 years old the day Junior made the team.

Years

entrance exam, he lost his concentration and ended up with a score of 690. It was 400 points below what he had expected. Worse, it was 10 points below the minimum score required to play college sports. Junior had blown it—he would have to sit out an entire year.

Junior worked hard in the classroom during his freshman year, and trained hard to keep in shape. He was declared eligible to play his sophomore year, but due to a pre-season ankle injury, his playing time dwindled to a few minutes a game. Finally, in Junior's third year at USC, he got a chance to show what he could do.

Right away, Trojan fans knew they had a very special player on their team. Junior's combination of speed, strength, and intelligence made him unstoppable. Wherever the ball-carrier ran, Junior was right there when a play had to be made. Opposing coaches marveled at his skill. One even called him the best college player he had ever seen. No one could stop Junior, and he was getting better every week. In his final five games, he sacked the quarterback 13 times! For his efforts, Junior was selected as USC's MVP. He also was voted to the All-PAC 10 Conference team and honored as an All-American.

In what would be his final college contest, Junior helped the Trojans beat the University of Michigan in the Rose Bowl. His dramatic quarterback sack in the final seconds sealed a 17–10 win for USC.

A few months later, Junior decided to skip his final college season and entered his name in the NFL draft. There was nothing he wanted more than to finish school, but his father had developed a serious heart condition and the family could not afford proper medical care. An NFL contract would take care of

During the 1989 season, Junior combined with linemen Tim Ryan (left) and Dan Owens (right) to record 45 quarterback sacks.

In only two active seasons at USC, Junior compiled impressive stats:

TACKLES

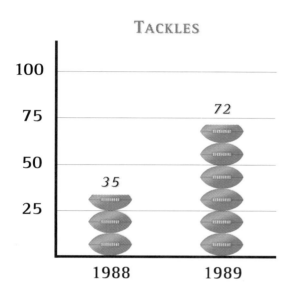

	1988	1989
	35	72

SACKS

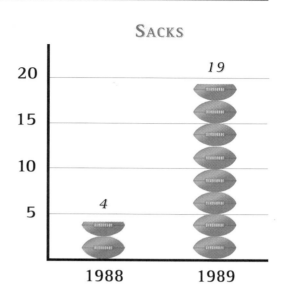

	1988	1989
	4	19

the family's money problems, and it would take Junior a step closer to his dream of becoming a pro football star.

"Turning pro was my way of saying to my father, 'You did all this for me, now I'll make you proud.'"

The Story

hen the San Diego Chargers planned their strategy for the 1990 NFL draft, they were sure of one thing: the team desperately needed an "impact" player. The Chargers had a group of good, young defenders, but no one stood out as a dominant force. When it was San Diego's turn to choose and Junior Seau was still available, general manager Bobby Beathard smiled. He knew the Chargers had gotten their man.

Junior pumps a fist in happiness as NFL commissioner Paul Tagliabue announces Junior as a 1990 first-round draft pick.

Continues

From the moment Junior pulled on the blue and gold Chargers uniform, he displayed the kind of intensity and courage that had been lacking in San Diego's players for nearly a decade. He inspired his teammates to give everything they had, to make the big play, and to hunger for winning.

When the 1992 season started, Junior believed the team was ready to come together. But after a month, the Chargers had no wins and four losses. No team had ever made the playoffs after such a horrible start. Yet deep down, Junior felt it could still be done. He raised his game to a new level, and teammates Leslie O'Neal, Chris Mims, and Stanley Richard responded to the challenge, too. The team won 11 of its final 12 games to capture the division title, and Junior was voted to the AFC All-Pro team for his inspiring performance.

Over the years, Junior has managed to maintain this exceptional level of play. In fact, he has become one of the most dominant linebackers in history. His knack for coming up with

Football experts compare Junior to all-time great linebackers Dick Butkus (above) and Lawrence Taylor (below).

big plays in big situations makes him one of the game's most exciting players. He has been compared to Hall of Famers such as Dick Butkus, Lawrence Taylor, and Mike Singletary for the controlled fury with which he attacks each play.

In 1994, Junior suffered a pinched nerve in his neck. Each time he made a tackle, he crumpled to the ground as white-hot pain flashed through his left shoulder and arm. But each time, he managed to pull himself up and continue playing. For a while, Junior lost much of the sensation in one of his arms, yet he remained a force on defense by hurling his body at ball-carriers to make tackles. When the Chargers made it to the playoffs, everyone wondered whether Junior could play. He answered that question in the AFC

Junior tackles Pittsburgh Steeler Ernie Mills during the AFC Championship Game.

Championship Game against the Pittsburgh Steelers. Junior turned in what many feel was the best single-game performance by a linebacker in the history of the playoffs. Junior propelled the Chargers to their first AFC championship and their first trip to the Super Bowl. On that unforgettable afternoon, Junior all but guaranteed his spot in the football Hall of Fame.

Timeline

1989: Voted PAC-10 Defensive Player of the Year

1992: Rallies San Diego Chargers from an 0–4 start to a berth in the AFC playoffs

1990: Stars in USC's 17–10 Rose Bowl win over Michigan

1994: Wins All-Pro honors for the third straight year

1995: Plays in Super Bowl XXIX against the San Francisco 49ers

1995: Leads San Diego to victory over Pittsburgh in the AFC Championship Game

Game

When teams prepare to play the Chargers, the first thing they make sure of is that Junior is blocked on every play. They know he is fast enough to make tackles anywhere on the field. Junior is always easy to spot on the field. His energy and great athletic ability stand out on almost every play.

Junior says he likes to make ball carriers "Say Ow" when he hits them. "Say Ow" is a pun on the pronounciation of "Seau."

Action!

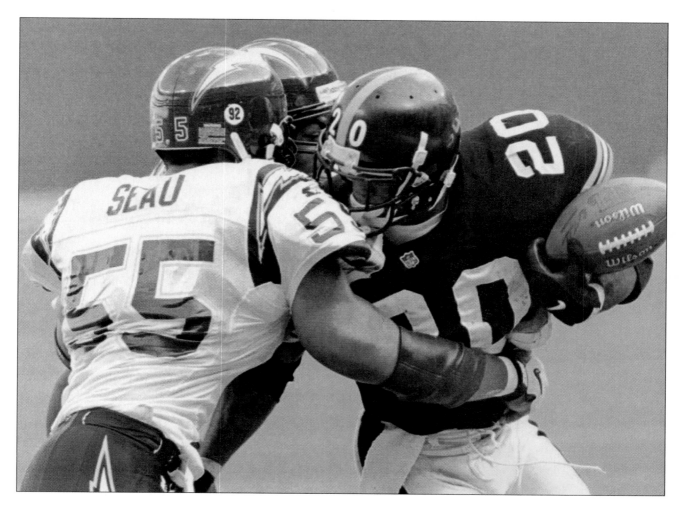

Junior jars the ball loose from Pittsburgh running back Eric Pegram.

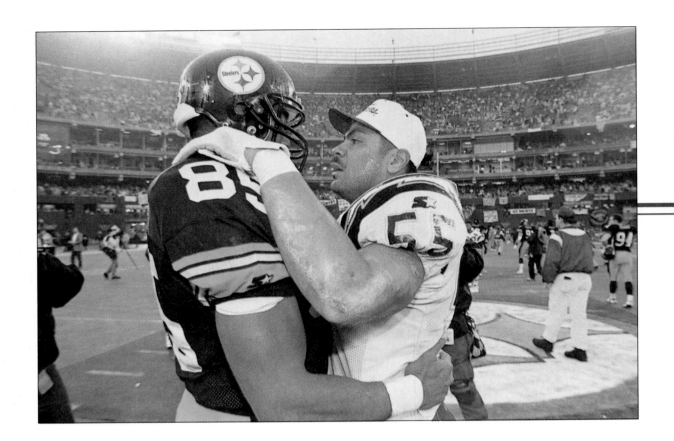

Junior played in blinding pain for much of the 1994 season. His courage inspired the Chargers to the AFC title.

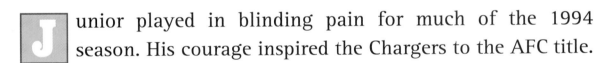

Junior is well prepared for every game. He loves anticipating the offense's play and then stopping it.

Junior plays so hard that he has earned the admiration of all his opponents. "I just hope that after I hang up my helmet, I'll be respected with the elite group."

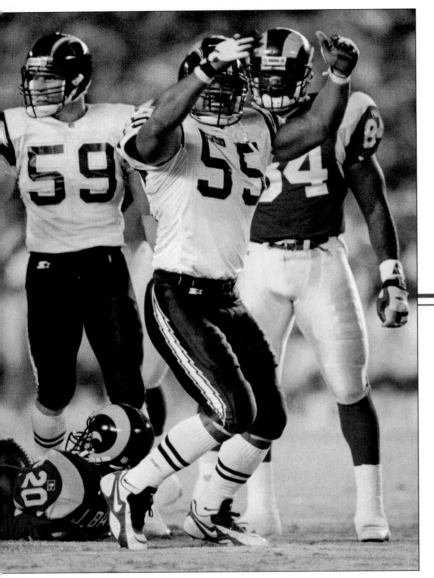

Sometimes Junior gets so pumped up on the field that he can barely control himself. His teammates call him the "Tasmanian Devil" after the famous cartoon character.

Says Junior, "No matter whether you win or lose, you have to be a good sport."

Junior's fans adore him. He gets more fan mail than any non-quarterback in the NFL.

Dealing

When Junior Seau messed up his SATs, it was the most humiliating experience of his life. Not being allowed to play football was bad enough. But he soon learned that he was the only student on the entire USC campus attending school on a special program called Proposition 48, which was meant to help students who did not live up to normal academic standards.

"Everything I had worked for—everything my family stood for—was gone. I was so embarrassed that I went back to Oceanside High and personally apologized to all of the teachers who had helped me. Then I decided to work hard all year and prove I wasn't a 'dumb jock.' By the end of my first year at USC, my grades were above average and I was ready to move forward."

Junior worked hard to improve his grades so that he could attend, and play football at, the University of Southern California.

With It

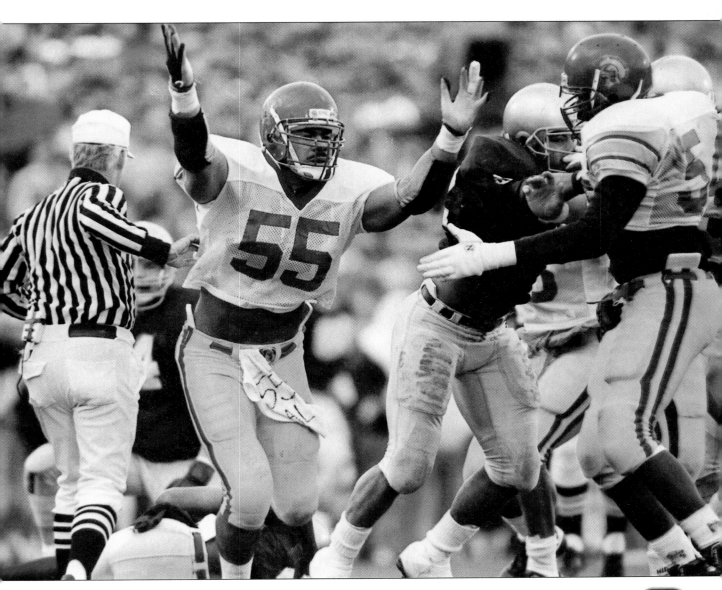

HOW DOES

Junior prepares for practice and games in the same manner—he studies hard, watches film, lifts weights, and stretches.

He Do It?

ost fans believe that Junior Seau is some sort of "wild man," whose only purpose is to create havoc. Junior's teammates know otherwise. He spends hours each day studying the next team the Chargers will face, and he memorizes as many of their plays as he can. Then he goes out and practices at full speed—something most NFL players do not like to do.

"I refuse to go into a Sunday game knowing that I didn't practice hard enough, study enough, or put in enough time in the weight room or the film room. When I get on the field, it should be easy—I should be able to anticipate everything that's going to happen. Everything."

The Grind

As one of football's most involved and outgoing players, Junior Seau faces the challenge of spending quality time with both his fans and his wife and children. He must also make time for his work with his charitable organization, the Junior Seau Foundation.

"The hardest thing about being a professional athlete is drawing the line between family and fans. Balancing the needs of both can be difficult."

Junior's wife, Gina, often brings their children, Sydney and J. R. to San Diego games. There they will join Junior's brothers, sisters, uncles, aunts, and cousins in the parking lot before the game for a traditional Samoan feast.

"Gina is my best friend. She's my rock. She supports me and is my stability."

Junior sits with daughter Sydney.

Say What?

What are football people saying about Junior Seau?

"We're never quite sure what he's going to do."

—*Burt Grossman,*
San Diego Chargers defensive end

"He's the guy we have to watch out for—he's the best."

—*Kevin Greene, Pittsburgh Steelers*

"I knew he was a great player, but it turns out he's even better off the field."

—*Shawn Lee,*
    San Diego Chargers defensive tackle

"What makes Junior special is that he has such great natural talent, yet he trains with a 'Rocky' mentality."

—*John Dunn, San Diego Chargers strength and conditioning coach*

"Seeing him play hurt, you tell yourself, 'I need to get out and start playing, because he's stepping it up.'"

—*Stanley Richard, San Diego Chargers safety*

"Playing with Junior is like stepping on the court with Michael Jordan."

—*Reuben Davis, San Diego Chargers defensive tackle*

Career

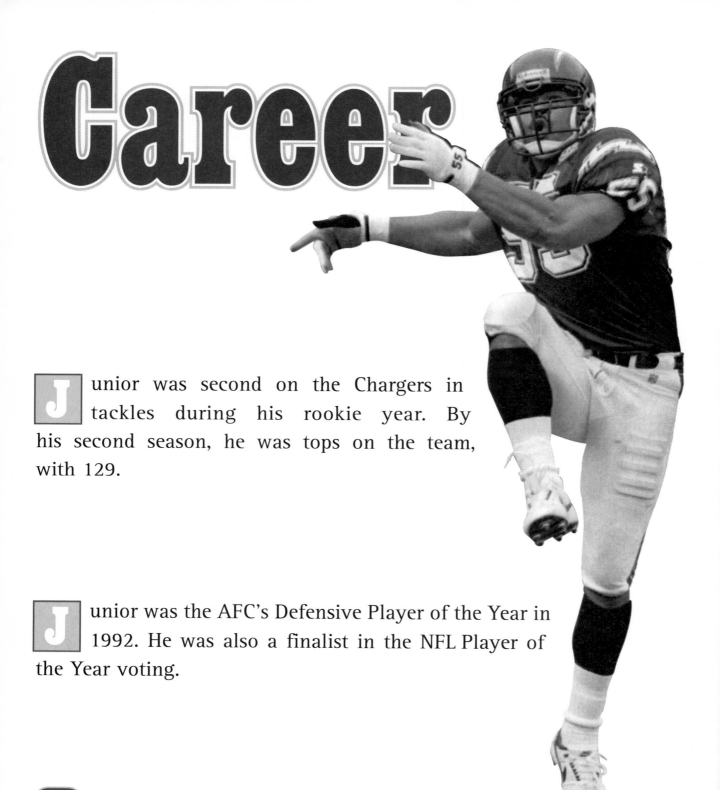

Junior was second on the Chargers in tackles during his rookie year. By his second season, he was tops on the team, with 129.

Junior was the AFC's Defensive Player of the Year in 1992. He was also a finalist in the NFL Player of the Year voting.

Highlights

T hough primarily a run-stopper and pass-rusher, Junior has intercepted six passes in his career, including two in 1995.

Junior makes a leaping interception in front of Indianapolis Colts receiver Bradford Banta.

Junior combines with Darrien Gordon to bring down Miami receiver O. J. McDuffie.

unior was honored as the NFL's Linebacker of the Year in 1993 and 1994.

unior made 19 tackles against the Miami Dolphins in a 22–21 playoff win in 1995. The following week, he got 16 more against the Pittsburgh Steelers in the AFC Championship Game.

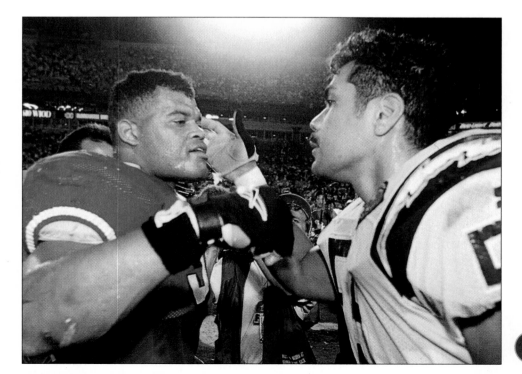

By making it to the Super Bowl in 1995, Junior (right) achieved one of his dreams.

Reaching

Out

In 1992, Junior Seau established a foundation to help kids. Since then, the Junior Seau Foundation has become a major force in the San Diego community. Junior throws himself into this work with the same go-for-broke style he displays on the football field. He spends hundreds of hours every year trying to keep children in school, off drugs, and out of gangs. Junior says he sees a little of himself in these troubled teens, and he also sees his youngest brother, Tony, who got involved with a gang when he was 15 and was sent to jail for his role in a 1993 turf war.

"The streets are tough and the influences of the 'hood are powerful. Everyone has to make their own decisions. You've got to decide whether you want something in your life and go after it, or just follow someone else's lead. I say be yourself—it's a lot easier!"

Numbers

Name: Tiaina Seau Jr.

Nickname: Junior

Born: January 19, 1969

Height: 6' 3"

Weight: 250 pounds

Uniform Number: 55

College: University of Southern California

Junior is at his best when the football is loose on the ground. He has recovered an opponent's fumble eight times in his career.

Year	Team	Games Played	Tackles	Sacks	Interceptions
1990	San Diego Chargers	16	85	1	0
1991	San Diego Chargers	16	129	7	0
1992	San Diego Chargers	15	102	4.5	2
1993	San Diego Chargers	16	129	0	2
1994	San Diego Chargers	16	155	5.5	0
1995	San Diego Chargers	16	129	2	2
Total		95	729	20	6

What If...

In football, your career can end at any moment. I've always known that, but I have never let myself think about it. It's also hard for me to look back and say what I'd be doing if I hadn't accomplished so much in football. It gave me the opportunity to go to college, where I studied the inner workings of cities and towns. What if I hadn't made it in the NFL? I might be working in urban planning, or maybe I'd be chasing some other dream. The one thing I've learned in life is that you have to have dreams, because no matter who you are or where you're growing up, dreams are for free. Dream about what you want to be, and then make it happen."

Glossary

ACADEMIC concerning education and learning

AMERICAN SAMOA Polynesian island group in the Pacific Ocean, located approximately halfway between Hawaii and Australia

BERTH a position; a slot

BLOSSOMED grew

COMPARISON an examination of likenesses and differences

DELICACIES foods that are rare, delicious, and usually expensive

DOMINANT the most powerful person or team

DWINDLE to waste away; to shrink

ELIGIBLE possessing the needed abilities to perform a task

PUBLIC ADMINISTRATION managing the affairs of government as they pertain to the people; public service

REQUIRED called for; needed

SCHOLARSHIP money given to a student to help pay for schooling

SPECIFIC focused on one particular thought or object

VERSATILE having the ability to excel in many different areas; multitalented

ELITE the best of the best; superior; upper class

HAVOC great confusion and destruction

KNACK a clever, natural talent

MARVEL to be full of surprise, wonder, and astonishment

MOTIVATE to excite and inspire

Index

About The Author

Mark Stewart grew up in New York City in the 1960s and 1970s– when the Mets, Jets, and Knicks all had championship teams. As a child, Mark read everything about sports he could lay his hands on. Today, he is one of the busiest sportswriters around. Since 1990, he has written close to 500 sports stories for kids, including profiles on more than 200 athletes, past and present. A graduate of Duke University, Mark served as senior editor of *Racquet*, a national tennis magazine, and was managing editor of *Super News*, a sporting goods industry newspaper. He is the author of every Grolier All-Pro Biography.